Wher
Jerusalem?

by Ellen Morgan

illustrated by Stephen Marchesi

Penguin Workshop

For Jane O'Connor,
an amazing editor and mentor—EM

PENGUIN WORKSHOP
An imprint of Penguin Random House LLC, New York

First published in the United States of America by Penguin Workshop,
an imprint of Penguin Random House LLC, New York, 2024

Visit us online at penguinrandomhouse.com.

Library of Congress Cataloging-in-Publication Data is available.

Printed in the United States of America

ISBN 9780593523506 (paperback)   10 9 8 7 6 5 4 3 2 1 WOR
ISBN 9780593523513 (library binding)   10 9 8 7 6 5 4 3 2 1 WOR

Contents

Where Is Jerusalem?

On December 21, 2008, just outside the walls of Jerusalem's Old City, a group of people were hard at work. They were looking for clues to Jerusalem's past. They dug with spades. They carted off dirt in buckets. They brushed away debris.

One of the people had come to Jerusalem on vacation. She was helping out at the dig for a month. While she was working by a wall of an old house that had fallen down in the 600s CE, she moved a large rock. Under it was a real-life treasure!

She, a tourist, had found 264 gold coins!

One side of each coin showed the face of an emperor. The other had a cross. At the time when the coins were made, Jerusalem was under Christian rule. The coins had probably been inside a niche in the wall. After the building fell down, the coins were buried. And there they remained, untouched, for 1,400 years.

Only a few years before this find, no one knew the spot of the dig was so special. It was an ordinary parking lot. Kids played soccer there when the lot was empty.

In 2005, the city had made plans to replace the parking lot with a large building and an underground garage. Soon after the work started, it came to a stop. While digging the garage, workers found remains of the ancient city. Out went the construction trucks. In came the archaeologists—scientists who learn about the past by digging it up.

Jerusalem is one of the oldest cities in the world. That accounts for why discoveries like this happen. Jerusalem is like a giant layer cake of history. The city has been destroyed and rebuilt many times. It was ruled by one empire after another, by Jewish kings, Roman governors, and Muslim leaders. New buildings were built on top of the ruins of old structures. New streets were laid over old ones; new buildings were constructed using stones from older ones.

A former parking lot is now the biggest active dig site in Jerusalem. Only fifty feet below where buses once parked are traces of what life was like more than a thousand years ago. One of the layers included a market from the ninth century CE.

Another had remains of a mansion that may have belonged to a queen. And below the mansion was a Roman villa from the first century!

The ancient city lies under the modern city. Jerusalem's history lies hidden below where people live and play and eat and walk every day.

In Jerusalem, secrets are just waiting for someone to find them.

CHAPTER 1
Old Versus New

Besides being one of the oldest cities in the world, Jerusalem is also one of the most important. It's located in Israel, a small, narrow country in the Middle East. On many old maps of Canaan—the area known today as Israel, Palestine, and Syria—Jerusalem is shown at the crossroads of Africa, Asia, and Europe.

This central location made it a city where people mingled, where trades were made, and where cultures collided.

Israel's government meets in Jerusalem. There is a court system, elected representatives, and a president. In the way the president of the United States lives at the White House in Washington, DC, Israel's president lives at the President's Residence in Jerusalem. The representatives meet in the Knesset.

The Knesset parliament building

Mountains and valleys in ancient Jerusalem

Jerusalem sits on a hill. Valleys surround it, with more hills climbing above the opposite sides of the valleys. Around one million people live there today, and even more come to visit. It draws over four million tourists a year.

Tucked within Jerusalem is the Old City, an area enclosed by walls that are fifty feet high and five hundred years old. Until the nineteenth century, just about everyone lived within the Old City. Its winding alleys and steep stairs make some people feel like they are in a maze.

Many streets are crooked and narrow. Buildings are made from the local rock. In fact, a modern law states that new buildings have to use this limestone. It's soft and white when it's first dug up. Over time, with sun and rain, the limestone becomes harder and turns a golden color. From afar, Jerusalem looks like a shining city on a hill.

The walls located around the Old City

The Old City is divided into four quarters. The Christian Quarter, the Muslim Quarter, and the Jewish Quarter got their name from the religions practiced by most of the people living in each quarter. The fourth quarter—the Armenian Quarter—is the smallest, with around two thousand residents. Their family roots originated in Armenia, a country about eight hundred miles northeast of Israel.

The Old City is small, less than half of one square mile. So, as more people came to live in Jerusalem, they settled outside the Old City to the west. This area—now called Modern Jerusalem—includes lots of restaurants, stores, clubs, and hotels.

Old and New

Jerusalem is an old city, but also modern. Old buildings stand near new luxury hotels, built to meet the demands of a booming tourist business. And in other parts of Israel, mostly near the coast, areas are known for electronics and the tech industry, while another area is known for an ancient profession, the diamond trade.

Most tourists come to Jerusalem to see the Old City. That is because the Old City is an important site for three of the world's oldest religions: Judaism, Christianity, and Islam. Three of their major holy sites dominate the landscape, rising above the rooftops.

Jewish people pray at the ancient Western Wall. Muslims flock to the Dome of the Rock, an Islamic shrine. Christians come to a huge complex known as the Church of the Holy Sepulchre.

Muslims, Jews, and Christians agree that Jerusalem is a holy city, a sacred place. Unfortunately, its long history has often been violent. It remains a place of unrest. Conflicts between followers of different religions sometimes end in bloodshed. The origin of the word *Jerusalem* is ancient and unclear, but one Hebrew translation is *City of Peace*. In today's world, peace often feels very far away.

Three Books

Judaism, Christianity, and Islam each have a holy book—the Torah, the Bible, and the Qur'an, respectively. The books share some of the same stories. Some of the same people, like Moses, Abraham, and David, appear in all three. All three religions believe in only one God. But there are some differences between these books and the beliefs of the people who read them.

The Torah contains God's teachings to the Jewish people. It begins with the creation of the world and ends with the death of Moses. A traditional Torah is handwritten on a scroll.

The Hebrew Bible includes the Torah as well as other books of Jewish writings and history, such as Job, Esther, and Psalms.

The Christian Bible has two sections. The Old Testament includes the Torah and tells of things that happened before Jesus was born. The New Testament tells the story of Jesus and his followers.

To Muslims, their holy book, the Qur'an, is the word of God. The angel Gabriel dictated it directly to the great prophet (teacher) Muhammad. The Qur'an contains prayers, history, and a promise of Paradise.

CHAPTER 2
The Long-Ago Past

More than five thousand years ago, nomads (people who normally moved from place to place) settled in the area that became Jerusalem. The land was dry and rocky. The summer months were hot and dry. The winters were cool. It was far from the coast and far from trade routes. Still, Jerusalem had two things going for it. Its high hills surrounded by deep valleys made it easy to defend. Also, a clear spring bubbled up nearby all year long. People needed the water both to drink and for crops, since not much rain fell in this area.

As the early settlement grew bigger, people built a high wall around it to keep themselves safe. The spring was just outside the wall, but they

carved a secret tunnel to the spring. Even if an
enemy attacked, they could still get to the water.

Water, Water

Water is scarce in a dry climate like Jerusalem's. In ancient times, people collected rainwater in cisterns—large tanks used for holding liquids— and sold it from the streets. Later, the Romans

built aqueducts to transport water from far away. The aqueducts worked so well, they were used for centuries. In fact, the plumbing system in Jerusalem didn't get upgraded until the twentieth century. Today, Israel is one of the world's best-practiced nations in managing and conserving water.

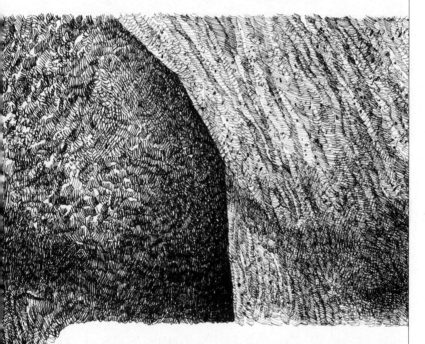

Ancient cistern discovered near the Temple Mount
in Jerusalem, present day

That plan, however, backfired when followers of the Jewish faith arrived around 1000 BCE. They had no settled home. Instead, they had been wandering in the desert for many years. Their leader was a man named David, who is part of all

David and his people arrive at Jerusalem

three religions. The Hebrew Bible says that King David found out about the secret tunnel to the spring. One of his men may have snuck through it and opened the gates to the well-defended city.

Jerusalem fell to David's army.

King David declared Jerusalem the capital of Israel, his kingdom. He bought the land at the highest point—around Mount Moriah—just north of the city and planned to put a Jewish temple there. David was a good king. He was a poet and a musician. But he was also a general and a warrior. He had fought battles and shed blood. According to the Hebrew Bible, God insisted that a man of peace—not a warrior—was the right person to build the Temple.

The Biblical account continues with David's son, Solomon. Solomon took over Israel when King David died. Known for his riches and wisdom, Solomon was a leader, but not a general or a soldier. Under Solomon, the city grew bigger.

King Solomon

David and Goliath

The Hebrew Bible, the Christian Bible, and the Qur'an all tell a well-known story about David when he was young. David's people were at war with another tribe. At one point, instead of a regular battle, the enemy tribe put forward their strongest man, Goliath, to fight someone on the Hebrew side. Goliath stood more than nine feet tall.

He carried a spear and wore thick armor. No one wanted to take him on. Then a young shepherd named David stepped forward. Although much smaller than Goliath, David was brave. With just a slingshot and a few stones, he brought the giant down.

Its population doubled. The kingdom became very wealthy. His ships sailed around the world and returned with gold and silver, ivory, peacocks, and monkeys. Solomon bought horses from Egypt and traded goods with the queen of Sheba.

The queen of Sheba visits King Solomon

Using King David's plans, Solomon hired skilled craftsmen to work on the Temple. It took thirty thousand men and seven years, but when it was completed, the Temple complex was a wonder.

The Hebrew Bible describes it in detail. The natural hill was leveled at the top and walls were built around the sides of the hillside to make it into a raised rectangular shape. This area served as a base for the Temple and its large courtyard. The Temple was ninety feet long, thirty feet wide, and about as tall as a five-story building. Tall bronze pillars stood at the entrance. Gold, silver, and cedar decorated the building inside and out.

The innermost room of Solomon's Temple was known as the Holy of Holies. This spot was so sacred that only one person was ever allowed to step through its doors—the high priest. And not every day, either. He could only enter once a year! The Holy of Holies housed the Ark of the Covenant, a gold-covered wooden chest. Inside it were the Ten Commandments, written on two stone tablets that God had given to Moses.

The Ark of the Covenant

Solomon's Temple became the center of Jewish life in Jerusalem. Its people came to pray and to celebrate holidays. Visitors from other towns also traveled to the Temple.

After Solomon's death, the time of prosperity ended, and the kingdom split in two—a northern kingdom and a southern kingdom. The northern part was known as Israel and the southern as Judah. Three hundred years later, in 586 BCE, an army from Babylon attacked Jerusalem.

It looted the city, stole sacred objects, and burned down the Temple. Around ten thousand people from Jerusalem were taken to Babylon as prisoners and enslaved.

Even in captivity, the Hebrew Bible says, the Jewish people vowed to rebuild the Temple. Only fifty years later, after the Babylonian Empire was

conquered, they returned to Jerusalem and stuck to their word. The Second Temple was built where the first had been, only it was much smaller. It was not until centuries later, around 20 BCE, that a king acting as a governor for the Roman Empire expanded this temple. He was called Herod the Great, and he had been raised in the Jewish faith.

Herod the Great

Herod doubled the size of the raised rectangular area, which followers of Judaism call the Temple Mount. It grew to thirty-five acres. He built massive walls to support the Temple Mount. Bridges and wide staircases connected it to the older city of Jerusalem. The Second Temple was lavish,

with gold and silver trim. Its walls glowed in the sunlight.

The Second Temple also had the Holy of Holies, but unlike in the First Temple, the room was mostly empty. Along with other sacred objects from the First Temple, the Ark vanished after the Babylonians attacked.

Like Solomon's Temple, the Second Temple did not last. Beginning in 66 CE, people in Jerusalem revolted against the Roman Empire.

They were sick of high taxes and brutal treatment. The Roman general Titus headed up an army to crush the uprising. After a five-month siege, Titus sacked the city and burned the Temple . . . for a second time.

Roman general Titus

Once again, the Jewish people vowed to rebuild it. But even after two thousand years, this has yet to happen.

ITALY

SYRIA

JERUSALEM

EGYPT

ROMAN EMPIRE

Roman Empire around 70 CE

CHAPTER 3
The Western Wall

To Jewish people today, the holiest part of Jerusalem is the Western Wall. Sixty feet tall and made of ancient limestone, it was one of the walls built by Herod the Great, where his Temple complex once stood. The Temple stood on a raised platform that was supported by the wall. Most Jewish historians believe the Western Wall was close to the burned-down Temple. That is why this site is so important in Judaism.

The exposed section of the Western Wall is about 160 feet long. The large stone blocks near the bottom date to Herod's time. Near the top, the stones are smaller. They were added centuries later. In fact, much of the Western

Wall actually lies underground! However, visitors can walk through tunnels that were built in the 1970s and 1980s.

Jewish people do not worship on the Temple Mount, which Muslims call the Noble Sanctuary. Instead, they pray, both day and night, at the Western Wall. It never closes. Many write notes on pieces of paper and slip them into the cracks in the stones that form the walls. They believe the wall and the Temple Mount are close to heaven, and God will pay special attention to these prayers and notes. Twice a year the notes are cleaned out and respectfully buried at the Mount of Olives, another holy site nearby.

Men, with their heads covered, pray on one end of the courtyard. Women pray on the other. Rabbis, who are Jewish religious teachers,

read the words of the Torah aloud. At certain times and on particular holidays, someone blows a ram's horn trumpet, called a shofar. People celebrate holidays in the plaza. No trees can be planted in the Western Wall courtyard until after the third and final Temple is built.

Shofar

Tight Spaces

The Western Wall plaza is much larger today than it once was. For centuries, only a tiny plaza was open in front of the wall. People squeezed into a space only about half the size of a singles tennis court to say prayers. All that changed in 1967 when Israeli government leaders bulldozed the buildings around this small space, including houses of Muslim people, to expand the plaza. Jewish people celebrated the bigger space, but the Arab families mourned their lost homes.

Prophet Muhammad's steed

The Western Wall is known by many names. In Hebrew, it's called *Ha-Kotel Ha-Ma'aravi*. That's often shortened to *Kotel*. Christians sometimes refer to the Western Wall as the Wailing Wall, since many people weep while they pray there. They are lamenting the loss of the Temple and the sorrows of history. To Muslims, the Western Wall is the *Buraq*. They believe that in 621 CE, Muhammad, the great prophet of Islam, tethered his steed, named al-Buraq, to the wall. Then he climbed up to the Noble Sanctuary and to heaven.

CHAPTER 4
A New Religion

Judaism is the oldest of the three main religions in Jerusalem. But soon after Herod completed the Second Temple, a new religion sprang up from Jewish roots. According to the Bible, a descendant of King David was born in Bethlehem, a town about six miles from Jerusalem. The baby's name was Jesus. When Jesus was a boy,

Baby Jesus, Mary, and Joseph

his Jewish parents, Joseph and Mary, took him to Jerusalem for the holiday of Passover. He visited the Second Temple and talked with the Jewish priests there. They were impressed with how much he knew about the Torah.

As Jesus got older, he began to preach. He preached about love and peace. He preached that everyone was equal, rich or poor. He preached that God was more important than the Roman rulers. People started to listen. Some believed he would free the Jewish people from their enemies.

Not everyone liked what Jesus had to say. Jewish leaders didn't agree with how his teachings differed from theirs. Many Romans worried that he might lead a revolt against the Roman Empire.

To stop this, the Romans arrested Jesus and sentenced him to death. The New Testament of the Christian Bible tells how Jesus died on a cross on a hill just outside the city. His followers, called disciples, entombed him in a cave. Three days later, some of his followers returned and found the tomb empty. There was no body inside the cave because Jesus had "risen from the dead!" they declared.

Jesus being arrested by the Romans

Many Gods

Unlike Muslims, Jews, and Christians, Romans didn't believe in a single all-knowing God. They believed in many gods. Jupiter was the king of the gods. His wife, the queen, was Juno. Neptune was the god of the sea, Venus the goddess of love, and Mars the god of war.

Jupiter and Juno

Minerva

The god of music and art was Apollo, and his sister, Minerva, was the goddess of wisdom. They were just a few of the many, many gods in which the Romans believed!

Jesus's followers did not forget him. They carried his words beyond Jerusalem and wrote them down in what would become the New Testament. What they shared wasn't Judaism anymore. It was a new religion—Christianity. They believed Jesus was the son of God, something Jewish people and Muslims do not believe (though Muslims do regard Jesus as an important prophet of God).

Killing Jesus did not end the unrest in Jerusalem. Decades after Jesus's death, the people of Jerusalem revolted. The Roman emperor sent an army to crush the rebellion. In 70 CE, General

Titus attacked and forced his way inside the city. This was when the Second Temple was burned. The army destroyed other buildings and pulled down the city walls. Thousands of people were killed.

Jerusalem lay in ruins for many years. Gradually, the Roman Empire started to rebuild it. Emperor Hadrian renamed the city Aelia Capitolina in 130 CE and created a new city.

Emperor Hadrian

It began to take on a Roman feel. The Romans laid down wide streets running north to south and east to west. They built theaters, two market forums, and an arena for events. They constructed the aqueducts, using gravity to channel water to the city. Roman-style public baths were added, too. Most homes back then didn't have bathrooms.

During this period, Emperor Hadrian banned Jewish people from living in the city. He changed the name of the land around the city to Syria Palaestina. Hadrian built a new temple where the Second Temple had stood. This temple was dedicated to Jupiter. Another temple was put up over the place where Jesus had been buried. Some historians think Hadrian purposely built there to cover up the holy site. He might have figured that Christians wouldn't want to pray by a temple to a Roman god.

Many Christians back then were arrested. Others were killed for their beliefs. Still they persisted, and the religion grew.

In 312 CE, Christianity found a champion.

That year, Constantine, a son of a Western Roman emperor, saw a cross of fire in the sky before an important battle. Constantine became both emperor and a Christian. He no longer believed in many Roman gods. He believed in only one, the God of David and Jesus.

Emperor Constantine

In 325, Constantine sent his mother, Helena, to Jerusalem. He wanted her to seek out the holy sites from the New Testament of the Bible. Helena was then in her seventies. She had become a Christian even before her son. In fact, she had told him all about the religion.

Helena, Emperor Constantine's mother

When Helena arrived in Jerusalem, she found the place where Jesus had died, a hill called Golgotha. People told her Jesus's tomb—or sepulchre—lay under the temple that the Romans had built. Helena got to work. She had that Roman temple torn down, as well as the temple to Jupiter on the Temple Mount. Where the First Temple had been, Helena built a church, the Church of the Holy Sepulchre.

Church of the Holy Sepulchre

The holiest part of the church was a large round space, or rotunda, around Jesus's tomb.

Helena marked other holy spots in Jerusalem with new churches. She collected relics from Jesus's life, like the cross he had died on. All the work sparked interest in the city. Christians began traveling there to see the places mentioned in the Bible. A trip to a holy place is called a pilgrimage, and the people who make one are called pilgrims.

Traveling from England or Spain or Italy to Jerusalem wasn't easy. Pilgrims had to carry their money with them to pay for food and places to stay. Sometimes thieves and outlaws attacked pilgrims on the way. Completing a pilgrimage to Jerusalem was a big deal for a Christian. Pilgrims felt that seeing where Jesus died and was buried would bring them closer to God.

As Christianity grew, the practice of worshipping many Roman gods died out. In 313, Constantine officially made Christianity legal throughout the Roman Empire. It became the official religion of the Roman Empire in 380.

Via Dolorosa

Via Dolorosa means the "Way of Pain." Christians believe it's the path that Jesus walked, carrying his own cross, through Jerusalem to the hill where he died. On Good Friday, the Friday before Easter Sunday, thousands of Christians follow what are thought to be Jesus's final steps.

CHAPTER 5
The Church of the Holy Sepulchre

Pilgrimages to Jerusalem still occur even now. People of today want to see where Jesus died and where he was buried. Some walk the Via Dolorosa through the Old City. It can get very hot.

The sun beats down. The streets are noisy. When people finally reach the Holy Sepulchre, they enter through thick doors. Inside the church, it's cooler, quieter, calmer.

The Church of the Holy Sepulchre that stands in Jerusalem now isn't the same church built in the fourth century CE. Most of that church was torn down after Muslims conquered the city centuries later. The cave where Jesus had been buried was also destroyed.

After hundreds of years, Christians got back control of Jerusalem, and they rebuilt the church. Some of the columns had survived. They kept these old columns and added new levels on top of them. They built a new dome soaring high above the site of the tomb. The rotunda became the heart of the new church.

The footprint of the church changed, too. The new Church of the Holy Sepulchre includes Golgotha within its walls.

The place where Jesus was buried is the holiest spot in the Church of the Holy Sepulchre. A small building inside the building, called an Edicule, protects the tomb. A tower tops the Edicule. Portholes pierce its sides. Visitors can look through these portholes to see Jesus's tomb. Visitors were not allowed to enter the Edicule, but that rule changed in 2017. Taking photographs inside the Edicule is not allowed, though.

The Church of the Holy Sepulchre is unusual in many ways. It's not a single building. It's more like a series of buildings and courtyards and chapels. It has several domes. Most churches in the world belong to only one religious group, but six different Christian groups— Greek Orthodox, Roman Catholic, Armenian Apostolic, Coptic, Syriac Orthodox, and Ethiopian—share the Church of the Holy Sepulchre. The most sacred parts are common property. Every group can use the rotunda, the Edicule, and the church entrance.

Very close to the Edicule is a small chapel with two ancient rock tombs. These date back to Jesus's time and look something like his tomb. Another tiny chapel at the back of the church supposedly lies directly under the spot where Jesus died.

Even the roof of the Church of the Holy Sepulchre is interesting. People live there! About twenty Ethiopian monks stay in small cells in a monastery that looks like some monasteries in Africa.

In order to make any changes to the church, all six groups have to agree. Sometimes that can be very hard to do. For instance, one ladder resting against a wall hasn't been moved in about three hundred years. The different groups can't agree on who put the ladder there and why. Or what should be done with it!

At times, fights have broken out in the Church of the Holy Sepulchre. But the different groups often get along. They believe in the same God. They believe in Jesus. And they all agree that the Church of the Holy Sepulchre is their most holy site.

CHAPTER 6
A New Prophet

By the seventh century CE, Jerusalem was a city of two religions, Judaism and Christianity. But a prophet, named Muhammad, soon brought a third religion to the holy city: Islam.

Muhammad lived in the city of Mecca, almost eight hundred miles southeast of Jerusalem.

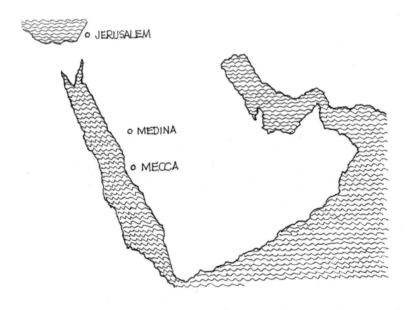

He was a shepherd and a merchant. A monk taught him Christianity, and he studied Jewish teachings, too. Muhammad claimed that in 610 CE, when he was forty years old, the angel Gabriel visited him. Gabriel told Muhammad that God, called Allah by Muslims, had picked him to be his messenger and prophet.

Muhammad shared Allah's words with other people. If they believed in Allah, they would be rewarded in heaven. His teachings had many things in common with the Bible and the Torah. In Islam, David, Solomon, and Jesus are known as prophets. Muhammad is the last prophet. What Gabriel told Muhammad built on the earlier lessons of Judaism and Christianity. Eventually his teachings were written down in the Qur'an.

One of the most famous stories about Muhammad is his Night Journey. According to the story, Gabriel woke up Muhammad one night.

Following the angel, Muhammad rode a magical horse, his steed al-Buraq, to the "farthest place of worship." Even though the Qur'an doesn't name it, Muslims agree this spot was Jerusalem. Muhammad hitched al-Buraq to the Western Wall. From the raised platform, Muhammad climbed a golden ladder of light up to heaven. He talked with other prophets, including Abraham and Jesus. He met Allah.

Because of Muhammad's Night Journey, Jerusalem is the third most holy city to Muslims. The holiest are Mecca and Medina, both in what today is Saudi Arabia. Mecca was where Muhammad was born. Medina is where he lived and worked to establish the new religion of Islam, based on his teachings and worship of Allah.

Muhammad died in 632 CE, but his followers continued to share his teachings. Islam spread very quickly across the Middle East and Africa. More and more people became Muslims. Around 637 CE, Muslims marched to Jerusalem. Leading them was Omar, the elected caliph, or successor to the prophet. Jerusalem surrendered to his army. On entering the city, Omar went to the Church of the Holy Sepulchre. Out of respect, he refused to pray there. He knew if he did, his followers might turn the church into a Muslim house of worship, a mosque, and he didn't want that to happen.

Next Omar asked to see the Temple Mount.

He found it neglected. The buildings were just ruins—and had been for hundreds of years. People threw their trash on the Temple Mount. Christian rulers hadn't allowed Jewish people to care for the sacred hilltop.

Omar cleaned up the garbage. Then, after clearing the hilltop of ruins, Muslims built a magnificent shrine, the Dome of the Rock, where the Jewish Temple had stood. Another mosque, al-Aqsa, was built at the southern end of the Temple Mount. Muslims began to call the raised area the Noble Sanctuary, or Haram al-Sharif.

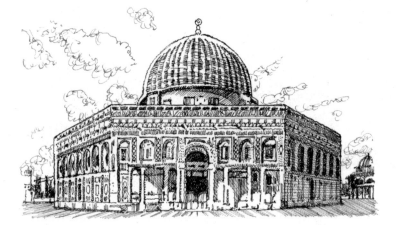

Dome of the Rock

Islamic Calendar

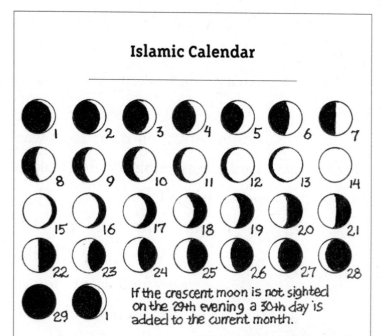

If the crescent moon is not sighted on the 29th evening a 30th day is added to the current month.

A year in the Islamic calendar has around 354 or 355 days, because it's based on the cycles of the moon. A calendar based on the sun, on the other hand, has 365 or 366 days. In the same way that Christians track years starting around the time when Jesus was born, the Muslim calendar begins on the year Muhammad went to the city of Medina, his Hijrah. It's AH 1 or the first Hijrah year. That means, to Muslims, the year AH 1421 began on April 6, 2000.

For the next few centuries, Jerusalem thrived. Muslims allowed Jewish people to worship at the Noble Sanctuary. They accepted Christians in the city, too. The three groups got along well. But in 1009, a different caliph came to power. Known for his extreme violence, Al-Hakim gave an order—destroy the Church of the Holy Sepulchre. And so it was.

Pope Urban II

Pope Urban II, the most important leader of the Roman Catholic Church, asked his followers to win back the lands of the Bible. An army of believers set out on a holy Crusade, a religious war. Many more followed. The goal was to regain the Holy Land, which included Jerusalem.

In 1099, the Crusaders from Western Europe

conquered Jerusalem. They showed no mercy to the people who lived there. They burned Jewish houses of worship with people inside them. They cut off the heads of Muslims. After two days of killings, hardly anyone was left alive.

The Crusaders set to work rebuilding the Church of the Holy Sepulchre. They turned the Dome of the Rock into a church. They added a huge cross on top of the Muslim shrine and put Christian statues and paintings inside.

With Jerusalem under Christian control again, many Christians all over Europe wanted to visit the holy city. A new religious order formed to help the pilgrims get to Jerusalem safely. The order's members were monks, but also soldiers. Many

had fought in the Crusades. The symbol of this new group was a red cross on a white background. They turned the al-Aqsa mosque on the Temple Mount into their headquarters, and the location gave them their name—the Knights of the Temple, or the Knights Templar.

But Christians did not hold on to Jerusalem for long—only around ninety years. In 1187, the Muslim warrior Saladin retook the city. In contrast to the brutal Crusader attack, he allowed Jewish people to come back to the city. He imprisoned Christians and let some of them buy their freedom.

Saladin took down the cross on the Dome of the Rock and removed the statues, but mostly left the Christian churches alone.

Saladin

A series of Muslim leaders ruled Jerusalem for centuries after Saladin's victory. Some built up the city walls. Others tore them down. They wanted to make sure that if invaders, such as the Crusaders, won the city again, the invaders could not barricade themselves inside. By 1270, the Crusades ended. After that, many Christians lost interest in Jerusalem. Christian pilgrimages dropped off.

Despite the centuries of fighting, the Crusades did cause a burst of trading among Christians and Arabs in Jerusalem. Silk, glass, and metal moved between Europe and Asia. Some of these goods ended up in Jerusalem markets.

The Silk Road

During the Middle Ages, the transfer of items between the East and the West often happened along what is known as the Silk Road. Despite its name, the Silk Road wasn't a single road. It was a network of trade routes, by land and sea, extending four thousand miles and connecting people from Asia, Africa, and Europe. Goods and ideas were traded, but sometimes diseases were exchanged, too. The Silk Road lasted from 130 BCE to 1453 CE, when the Ottoman Empire closed off trade with the West.

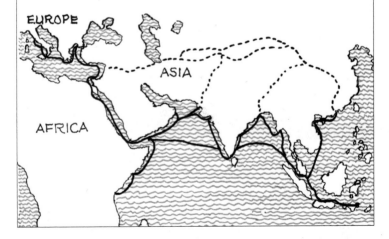

In 1516, Jerusalem became part of a huge Muslim-led empire known as the Ottoman Empire. Its most famous ruler, Suleiman, altered the city in important ways. He spiffed up the outside of the Dome of the Rock, replacing mosaics with colored tiles. He improved Jerusalem's water supply. Most importantly, he built a massive wall around the city. New sections of the wall rose up from the remains of earlier walls. Suleiman's wall was two miles long and forty feet high. It had thirty-four towers and seven gates. (An eighth gate was added later.)

That's the wall that still stands today. It's one of the city's most distinctive features. The gates people walked through during Suleiman's time are the same gates people walk through now, centuries later.

CHAPTER 7
The Dome of the Rock

The oldest surviving Muslim monument in the world is the blue-and-gold Dome of the Rock. Finished in 691 CE, it was built only a few decades after the death of the Prophet Muhammad. Over time, the outside has changed. Suleiman replaced the mosaics with tiles. A new dome had to be built after an earthquake. But the inside probably looks very similar to how it did in the seventh century.

One reason it's survived so long: It's literally built

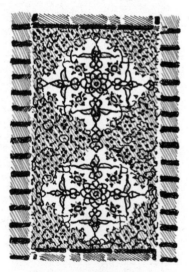

Tiles from the
Dome of the Rock

on a rock. It was constructed over an outcrop of stone on the highest natural point of the Temple Mount. In fact, it's probably the same stone on which the Jewish Temple was built. When Muslim visitors enter the Dome of the Rock, that's what they see—a part of the massive rough stone sticking up through the floor. A staircase leads down to a grotto under the rock, too.

Muslims believe the Rock is the closest they can get to heaven. In Islamic tradition, it marks the spot where Muhammad climbed a ladder of light to heaven on his famous Night Journey. They point to a footprint in the rock that they believe the Prophet Muhammad left behind.

The enormous rough stone sits in the middle of the shrine under the dome. The building that houses it is beautifully ornate. Stained glass fills the windows. Marble columns with gold tops circle the rock's rotunda, and arches connect the columns. Colorful mosaics decorate the marble walls. Words from the Qur'an adorn the building, too. The text runs more than seven hundred feet! A springy carpet covers the floor. Muslims can kneel and pray anywhere inside the Dome of the Rock.

The Dome of the Rock is beautiful inside and out. The building's shape is an octagon. It has eight sides and four doors. Blue tilework decorates the outside walls and a huge gold-plated dome sits on top. This gold dome dominates Jerusalem's skyline. Sixty-five feet in diameter, it's the same size as the large dome at the Church of the Holy Sepulchre, but two things make it more noticeable. Covered in thin sheets of gold, the dome is bright and eye-catching, especially when the sun shines on it. The dome also towers above other parts of the Old City. The Dome of the Rock stands on the raised area of ground that Herod built to support the Second Temple.

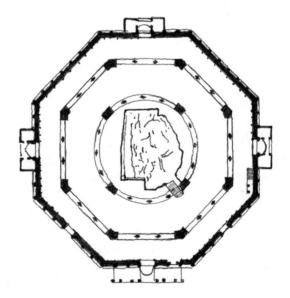

Jewish people call the large raised area the Temple Mount. Muslims call it the Noble Sanctuary. It's about the size of thirty football fields. The Noble Sanctuary has gardens, paths, trees, and other buildings. On its southern end is the al-Aqsa mosque, which has a silver dome.

Al-Aqsa mosque is a Friday mosque. That means Muslims gather there to pray at noon on Fridays, Islam's holiest day. The Dome of the Rock, on the other hand, isn't a mosque. It's considered a monument or a shrine. It enshrines the rock where Muhammad climbed to heaven.

The Rock

The rock inside the Dome of the Rock is sacred to all three religions. Many people think it's where God created Adam, the first person in the Bible. To Muslims, this is where the Prophet Muhammad climbed a ladder to heaven on his Night Journey. In Jewish and Christian tradition, Abraham came close to sacrificing his son Isaac here. Muslims believe something similar. Instead of Isaac, though, they believe Abraham's son Ismail was bound to this spot. And, of course, the rock is holy in the Jewish faith because it's where the Jewish Temple stood. Only Muslims are allowed inside the Dome of the Rock.

Muslims pray five times a day. When the call to prayer sounds, Muslims ready themselves. In the Old City of Jerusalem, many Muslims hurry toward the Noble Sanctuary or the al-Aqsa mosque. Others, like shopkeepers, aren't able to get to a mosque. They stop whatever they are doing. They wash their hands and face. They take off their shoes. They kneel on a prayer rug and bow toward Mecca, where Muhammad was born. After praying, everyone goes back to what they had left off doing, until the next call to prayer.

The Five Pillars of Islam

Muslims believe Allah gave Muhammad instructions in heaven. These are the Five Pillars, or main beliefs, of Islam.

1) One God. There is only one God—Allah—and Muhammad is his prophet.

2) Prayer. Muslims must pray five times a day.

3) Charity. Muslims must give to the poor.

4) Fasting. Muslims must fast from sunrise to sunset during the month of Ramadan.

5) Hajj. If a Muslim is rich enough, they must travel to Mecca at least once during their lifetime.

Like some Jewish people and Christians, Muslims believe that when the end of the world comes, it will happen in Jerusalem. On several sides of the Dome of the Rock stand a series of arches, that Muslims call the Scales. They think the scales of judgment will hang from the arches, and people's deeds will be weighed on the scales. If a person has been good enough, they will go to paradise. They may even meet Muhammad.

CHAPTER 8
Israel

For a long time, the city of Jerusalem was pretty much ignored outside the Ottoman Empire.

Other parts of the world kept changing. For centuries, some groups of people behaved cruelly to followers of the Jewish faith, and that bad behavior grew. By the late 1800s, across Europe and Asia, many people unfairly blamed Jewish people for their problems. In Russia, Jewish people were accused of causing unrest in the country. They were oppressed, killed, or forced to leave. But where could they go?

Many traveled to Jerusalem. A new movement started, called Zionism, after Mount Zion, the large hill just outside the walls of the Old City. Zionism's goal was to return Jewish people to their

Theodor Herzl

ancient homeland. Theodor Herzl, Zionism's founder, argued that Jews needed their own country—and Jerusalem should be its capital. Some Christians supported the movement. But not many.

Then, in 1914, Germany and its allies started a four-year war: World War I. It spread across much of the globe and ended in 1918 with Germany's surrender. During the war, the Ottoman Empire collapsed, and Great Britain came into control of Jerusalem. Centuries of Muslim rule ended.

In 1933, Adolf Hitler came to power in Germany. He blamed Jewish people for the loss of World War I. He wanted to wipe out anyone who practiced or was born into the religion. To escape, many German Jews fled to Jerusalem and the area around the city, what Emperor Hadrian had called Syria Palaestina. Now known as Palestine, it was the land between the Mediterranean Sea and the Jordan River. Jewish people considered this the land of their ancestors, as written in the Torah. The almost one million Arabs who already lived there considered it their home.

Hitler started World War II in 1939, and during the six-year war, murdered six million ordinary Jewish men, women, and children as well as more than five million more people whom Hitler considered enemies. Germany was defeated again, with Hitler taking his own life in the last days of the war. Now Zionists began to push harder than ever for a homeland. A place where they could be safe.

After World War II, many people in Jerusalem protested against British control. Finally, Great Britain agreed to give up its stake in the region. But who would get what?

Yad Vashem

In West Jerusalem on the slope of a mountain stands Yad Vashem, a museum and memorial established by the Knesset in 1953. Outside, the grounds have gardens and statues. The inside of the museum displays photos, documents, and things that belonged to people who died because of antisemitism, a hatred of Jewish people. The mission of Yad Vashem is to honor the millions of Jewish people murdered during World War II. This mass killing is known as the Holocaust.

In 1947, the United Nations, an organization made of representatives from countries around the world, stepped in. They divided the land known as Palestine into two states— an Arab state and a Jewish state. Jerusalem didn't belong to either.

No one seemed to like this solution. Fighting broke out after a few days. When the time came for the British to leave a few months later, in May 1948, Israel declared itself an independent nation with Jerusalem as the capital. This made many Arab people angry. They felt their land had been taken away from them without their consent.

Arab armies attacked right away. The brand-new Israeli army fought back. After many months, the two sides drew up a truce. It divided the city of Jerusalem in half. West Jerusalem—the new part of the city—became the capital of Israel.

East Jerusalem—the Old City—belonged to the Arabs. So Jewish people finally had a homeland, but for the first time in centuries, they could not worship at the Western Wall. They couldn't enter the Old City. Barbed wire, walls, and bunkers lined this new border.

As for the Arabs, they weren't happy, either. Many were forced out of their homes. Others fled. Around 700,000 left the region. They call the War of 1948 "the catastrophe." Meanwhile around 700,000 Jewish people moved in from other parts of the world. Israel became a refuge for Jewish survivors of World War II.

However, Israel was surrounded on all sides by much larger Arab states—Egypt, Syria, and Jordan. The tensions between Arabs and Israel increased. In June 1967, war erupted. The Six-Day War between Israel and the Arab states lasted less than one week. After surprise attacks on its rivals' air forces, Israel seized land from Egypt, Jordan, and Syria. Many people who lived there fled, and Israel forced out others. The fighting extended to Jerusalem. Bullets from this war pockmark one of the city's gates.

During the Six-Day War, Israel captured the Old City. Nineteen years had passed since Jewish people had last been able to pray at the Western Wall. It was a victory for Israel, but the underlying tensions were not solved.

Jewish people see Israel as their historic homeland. They look back to King David and King Solomon. They remember the two Temples.

They point to ancient ruins under Jerusalem. They do not forget how badly they were treated by occupying forces and how their homeland was taken from them over and over again.

However, Muslims and many Arabs view Palestine, which includes part of Israel, as their country. They do not forget how many Muslims were forced out of Israel after the war of 1948 and the Six-Day War. Even today, the Israeli government sometimes takes homes from Muslim families. Many Muslims feel they are treated as second-class citizens in Israel.

Jerusalem was a Jewish city before Muhammad was born. Jewish people controlled it for one thousand years. Muslims ruled it longer, 1,300 years, and more recently. Both Israel and Palestine have strong claims to the city and the surrounding land. That's why so much fighting occurs around this area. It's a problem that doesn't seem to have an answer that will satisfy both sides.

Palestine

Palestine is not currently a country, though many other countries recognize it as an independent state. It includes parts of Israel, the Gaza Strip, and the West Bank of the Jordan River. It's sacred to Jewish people, Muslims, and Christians and contains sites important in all three religions. Many Arab people call Palestine home and want to have this land returned to them.

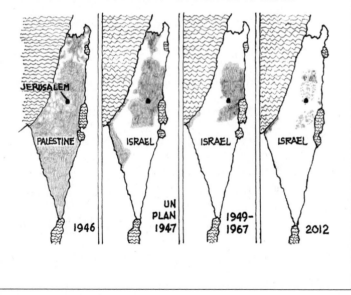

CHAPTER 9
Layer Cake

Parts of Jerusalem's Old City today aren't all that different from the way they were hundreds of years ago. There are no cars, for one thing. The same stone buildings crowd the narrow streets. In the Muslim Quarter, people shop at souks, or covered markets. They buy fruits, vegetables, spices, sweets, leatherwork, carved olive wood, and jewelry, just as people did for a thousand years before them. Christian monks walk through the city wearing religious robes. Muslim women cover their hair or faces. Some Jewish men dress in formal, traditional clothes.

But Jerusalem is modern, too, with tourists seeing as many people in jeans and T-shirts as in traditional outfits. There are churches, mosques, and religious sites, but visitors also go to the zoo or get french fries at McDonald's. It's a city that keeps changing. What people know about the city changes, too. New discoveries shift the perception of Jerusalem's past.

Despite its name, the Old City is not the oldest part of the city. King David didn't live there. The city he built doesn't lie within the current city walls. His capital and palace were just to the south.

In 2005, archaeologist Dr. Eilat Mazar found something that excited many people in Jerusalem. She claimed that the remains of a large ancient building south of the Old City were King David's palace. Later, her team uncovered thirty-six gold coins and a large gold medallion decorated with Jewish symbols. Incredibly, they also dug up three clay seal impressions with names they recognized. These same people were mentioned in the Hebrew Bible!

The history of Jerusalem doesn't belong only to Jewish people. Archaeologists have dug up Roman villas with mosaic floors and frescoes on the walls. They found a grand stepped stone avenue that once led to the Second Temple. They unearthed houses with baths—and even a 2,700-year-old toilet!

Stones laid during Herod's time were reused

by Hadrian, by Muslims, and by Crusaders in building arches, churches, and temples. Under the southeastern corner of the Noble Sanctuary lies a large vaulted hall known to many people as Solomon's Stables. It's not from the time of Solomon—Herod probably built this underground area when he doubled the size of the raised area for the expansion of the Second Temple. The pillars and arched vaults helped support the buildings above and relieved pressure on the outer walls.

During Herod's time, people may have used the space as a storage area for the Second Temple. After the Crusader conquest in 1099, Christian knights kept their horses there. Large iron rings where Crusaders tied the horses still remain on some of the pillars. Now Solomon's Stables is a Muslim prayer hall, known as the al-Marwani mosque. At this one site, as at many others, Jewish, Muslim, and Christian history mix together.

The layers of history are just one thing that makes Jerusalem truly unique. Everywhere, the stones of its walls and buildings show the city's age. But other parts of the past still lie tucked away under the present. Ancient beliefs mingle with modern inventions. Hundreds of thousands of citizens go about their lives every day, walking where kings once ruled, where warriors once fought, and where prophets once spoke.

In Jerusalem, the past is never far away.

Timeline of Jerusalem

c. 3000 BCE	Jerusalem is founded
c. 1000 BCE	King David's reign begins
c. 957 BCE	King Solomon completes the Temple
586 BCE	Babylonians conquer Jerusalem, destroy Solomon's Temple
63 BCE	The Roman Empire takes control of Jerusalem
66 CE	A Jewish revolt against the Roman Empire begins
70	The Romans lay siege to Jerusalem
130	Jerusalem renamed Aelia Capitolina by Hadrian
326	Emperor Constantine's mother, Helena, builds the Church of the Holy Sepulchre
637	Muslim forces under Omar conquer Jerusalem
688	Muslims begin building the Dome of the Rock
1099	Christian Crusaders conquer Jerusalem
1187	Saladin and Muslim forces retake Jerusalem
1270	Crusades end
1530s	Suleiman rebuilds Jerusalem's city walls and gates
1917	The British Empire takes control of Jerusalem
1948	Israel created after British withdrawal
1967	The Six-Day War takes place in June
2007	Excavation of Givati parking lot begins

Timeline of the World

c. 1200 BCE	Iron Age starts
753 BCE	Rome is founded
200 BCE	Paper invented in China
79 CE	Mount Vesuvius erupts
525	Anno Domini calendar invented
800	Charlemagne crowned Holy Roman Emperor
c. 1040	Invention of movable type in China
1347	Black Death plague begins in Europe
1439	Johannes Gutenberg invents the printing press
1564	William Shakespeare is born
1653	The Taj Mahal is completed in India
1789	The French Revolution begins
1820	Antarctica discovered by a Russian expedition
1861	The American Civil War begins
1896	First modern Olympic Games held in Athens, Greece
1905	Albert Einstein's Special Theory of Relativity published
1912	The Republic of China established
1953	Elizabeth II crowned queen of Great Britain
1992	Astronaut Mae Jemison becomes first African American woman in space

Bibliography

*Books for young readers

Biddle, Martin, Gideon Avni, Jon Seligman, and Tamar Winter.
The Church of the Holy Sepulchre. New York: Rizzoli, 2000.

Carroll, James. *Jerusalem, Jerusalem*. New York: Houghton
Mifflin, 2011.

Lawler, Andrew. *Under Jerusalem: The Buried History of the
World's Most Contested City*. New York: Doubleday, 2021.

Lemire, Vincent, Katell Berthelot, Julien Loiseau, and Yann Potin.
Jerusalem: History of a Global City. Translated by Juliana
Froggatt. Oakland: University of California Press, 2022.

Montefiore, Simon Sebag. *Jerusalem: The Biography*. New York:
Knopf, 2011.

*Morgan, Ellen. *Who Was Jesus?* New York: Penguin Workshop,
2015.

*Rechner, Amy. *Israel*. Minneapolis: Bellweather Media, 2018.

*Washburn, Kim. *Jerusalem*. Grand Rapids, MI: Zonderkidz, 2014.

*Young, Emma. *Israel*. Washington, DC: National Geographic,
2008.